Brock's Flock

by Liza Charlesworth • illustrated by Kelly Kennedy

SCHOLASTIC INC.

New York • Toronto • London • Auckland • Sydney
Mexico City • New Delhi • Hong Kong • Buenos Aires

Designed by Grafica, Inc.
ISBN: 978-0-545-68617-4
Copyright © 2009 by Lefty's Editorial Services.
All rights reserved. Published by Scholastic Inc.
SCHOLASTIC, LET'S LEARN READERS™, and associated logos are trademarks and/or registered trademarks of Scholastic Inc.

12 11 10 9 8 7 6 5 4 3 2 1   14 15 16 17 18 19/0

Printed in China.

What Is a Word Family?

A word family is a group of words that rhyme and share the same spelling pattern, such as *Brock*, *flock*, and *shock*. Read this story to learn more *-ock* words!

Meet **Brock**.
Brock is a member of the **Ock** family.

Now meet **Brock**'s **flock**.
Are you ready for a **shock**?

The **flock** lives next to **Brock**
in a giant **sock**.

What a **shock**!

The **flock** works in a **clock** shop with **Brock**'s pop.

What a **shock**!

The **flock** wears paint **smock**s
to pedal down the **block**.

What a **shock**!

The **flock** tells **knock-knock** jokes down at the **dock**.

What a **shock**!

But what is the biggest **shock**
about **Brock**'s **flock**?

That funky **flock** can really **rock**!

Word Family House

Point to the *-ock* word in each room and read it aloud.

dock	mock	lock
tock	rock	sock
block	Brock	stock
smock		knock
shock		flock

Word Family Match

Read each definition. Then go to the sock and put your finger on the right -*ock* word.

Definitions

1 a place for parking boats

2 a group of sheep

3 a tool for telling time

4 a stone

5 a type of apron

rock

flock

smock

dock

clock

-ock words

Word Family Maze

Help Brock find his flock. Put your finger on BEGIN. Then follow the trail of -*ock* words to get to the END.

BEGIN

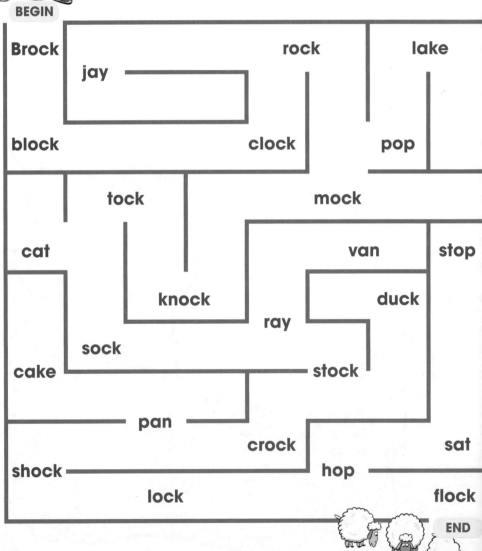

Brock   rock   lake

jay

block   clock   pop

tock   mock

cat   van   stop

knock   duck

ray

sock

cake   stock

pan

crock   sat

shock   hop

lock   flock

END